The first time I saw a swimmer hit a shark on the nose with a camera was in 1956. I was working at the BBC when a film editor burst in excitedly from the room next door. He asked me to come and look at something special. There, on the flickering screen of his editing machine, was the image of a huge shark. He pressed a button. The shark came to life and swam directly towards the camera. I could see rows of white triangular teeth lining its jaws. It came closer and closer until its head filled the screen – the camera jolted – there was a brief glimpse of grey flank – and the shark disappeared into blackness.

The film had been shot in the Red Sea, by a young Viennese biologist named Hans Hass. Hans was shooting the first-ever underwater series made by the BBC. And when it reached the television screen, it was a sensation. Much has changed since then: underwater cameras have become smaller and smaller, and now they can record hours of material before they need reloading. They are so sensitive that they can record pictures deep under the waves, far beyond the reach of the sun's rays, where the only light is that produced by deep-sea creatures in the pitch-blackness. Now, there is virtually no part of the seas that we cannot explore.

So, at the end of the millennium, teams from the BBC's Natural History unit began work on a series called *Blue Planet*. Its success was overwhelming, but no single series could hope to completely cover the undersea world. And now that we could take cameras into almost any part of the seas, could we discover new stories?

We have journeyed across the globe from the warm water of the tropics to the coldest around the Poles, to explore how life is lived beneath the waves. Underwater cameras have changed a great deal since that first shark bumped its nose on a camera, but our Blue Planet still holds extraordinary animals. It is a place of wonder and fragility. There is much to learn and much to protect. So, stand by for *Blue Planet II* and marvels beyond your imagining.

– SIR DAVID ATTENBOROUGH

BLUE
PLANET
II

PUFFIN BOOKS

UK | USA | Canada | Ireland | Australia | India | New Zealand | South Africa

Puffin Books is part of the Penguin Random House group of companies whose addresses can be found at global.penguinrandomhouse.com.

www.penguin.co.uk   www.puffin.co.uk   www.ladybird.co.uk

Penguin Random House UK

First published 2020
002

Written by Leisa Stewart-Sharpe
Text copyright © Children's Character Books Ltd, 2020
Illustration copyright © Emily Dove, 2020
Introduction copyright © David Attenborough, 2020
BBC and BBC Earth (word marks and logos) are trade marks of the British Broadcasting Corporation and are used under licence
BBC logo © 1996, BBC Earth logo © 2014

The moral right of the illustrator has been asserted
Produced in consultation with the Blue Planet II production team at BBC Studios Natural History Unit

Printed in Italy
A CIP catalogue record for this book is available from the British Library
ISBN: 978–1–405–94658–2

All correspondence to: Puffin Books, Penguin Random House Children's
One Embassy Gardens, 8 Viaduct Gardens, London SW11 7BW

MIX
Paper from responsible sources
FSC® C018179

THIS IS PLANET EARTH

A beautiful blue marble suspended in a sea of stars. Unlike billions of other planets in the Milky Way, 71 per cent of Earth is covered by ocean.

It's home to the greatest diversity of life on Earth but is our least explored habitat; we have better maps of Mars than of the ocean floor.

Although there's still so much to learn and more than a million species to discover, we know that oceans power this Blue Planet, our only home. Tiny marine plants produce over half of the world's oxygen, the ocean absorbs carbon dioxide gases that make our planet warmer, and billions of people depend on marine life to sustain their own. If our oceans don't thrive, neither will we.

So join us as we journey through our Blue Planet. Venture to The Deep, where creatures beyond your wildest imagination live in the dark. Explore coral reefs that shimmer in a kaleidoscope of colours. Peek past the tangled roots and fronds of our green seas. Join the commotion of our coasts, where rockpools have rush hours. Then leave the hustle and bustle far behind, for the wide open waters of the Big Blue.

Read on to discover all there is to love about our Blue Planet, and what you can do to protect this wilderness beneath the waves.

ONE OCEAN

There are great forces at work in our ocean. In this place of constant movement and change, tides tug, currents swirl and waves crash. Yet another growing force – climate change – is altering our Blue Planet at a faster rate than ever before in human history.

GO WITH THE FLOW
It's all one ocean, with everything connected by the global ocean conveyor belt. In the same way that blood is pumped around our bodies, this network of deep currents works as the ocean's circulatory system, slowly moving heat and food across the planet. Cold, nutrient-rich waters sink into the deep, where they spread across the ocean. They're replaced by warm surface waters which are carried from the Equator to the Poles. This creates a climate that's favourable for life.

TIDAL TUG OF WAR
The ocean rises and falls twice a day as Earth rotates. The side of Earth closest to the Moon bulges as the Moon's gravity pulls the ocean towards it. This raises the sea level and creates a high tide. At the same time, on the side of Earth furthest from the Moon, the ocean is pulled away from Earth's centre, creating another high tide. In the places inbetween, sea levels drop, which creates low tide.

MAKING WAVES
Waves gather strength as they roll in from far out at sea. They surge and grow before toppling in a thunderous cloud of salt spray. Waves have been recorded reaching ten storeys high (over 30 metres).

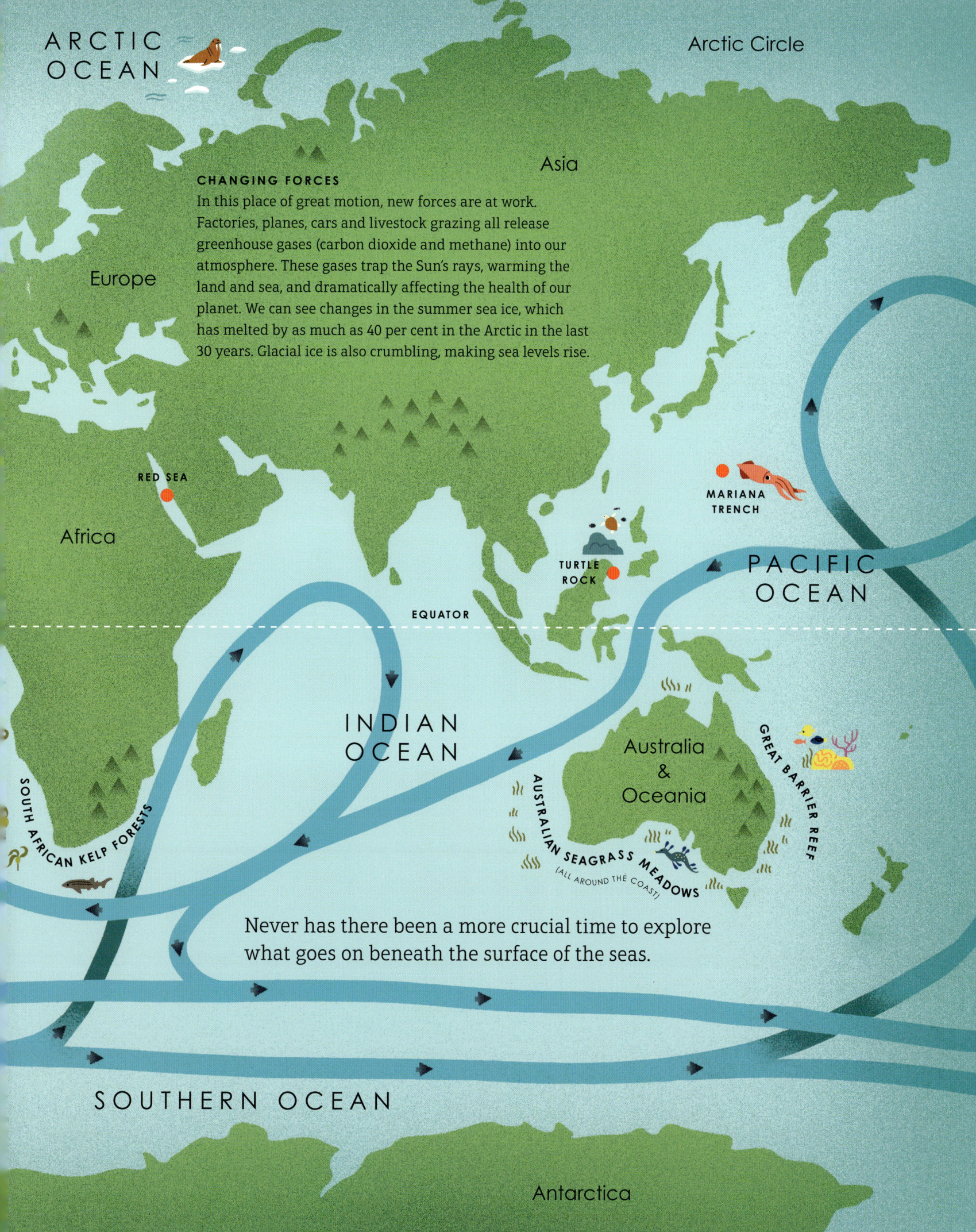

THE DEEP
THE EDGE OF THE UNKNOWN

Far beyond the reach of the Sun, an alien world hides beneath the waves. Welcome to The Deep. In this strange but true world, fish have feet and animals may go for a year without food. Incredibly, there's more life here than anywhere else on Earth. So take a deep breath, and dive into The Deep . . .

The Deep is so vast, it's bigger than all of Earth's other habitats combined. Below the sunlit shallows is the edge of the unknown – the **TWILIGHT ZONE**. It's dim, cold, and has crushing pressure. How could *anything* survive?

But just as the last of the light disappears . . . there's a glimmer in the gloom. Giant **HUMBOLDT SQUID** flash from white to red, striking with powerful suckers before disappearing in an inky smokescreen. And they're not alone: incredibly, 90 per cent of the ocean's fish call the Twilight Zone home.

LANTERNFISH

SWORDFISH

PYROSOME

HUMBOLDT SQUID

In the **MIDNIGHT ZONE** there are creatures that wouldn't be out of place in your nightmares, like this fearsome **FANGTOOTH**, which can gobble up a fish a third its size. Yet deep in this place of eternal darkness, many creatures make their own light through bioluminescence (*bye-oh-loo-mi-ness-ens*). They sparkle and swirl, putting on deep-sea firework displays.

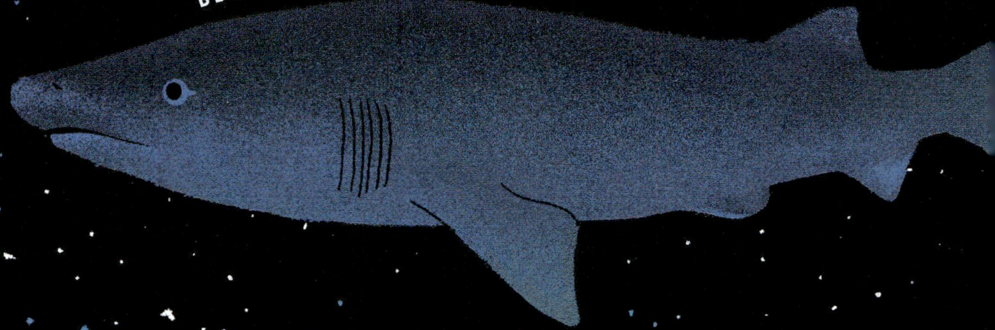

BLUNTNOSE SIXGILL SHARK

FANGTOOTH

JELLYFISH

SEA CUCUMBER

Marine debris falls like snow, feeding everything from **JELLYFISH** to **SEA CUCUMBERS** that open like umbrellas. What's left settles on the seafloor in the **ABYSSAL ZONE** (*ah-biss-sil*).

But this is *not* yet the bottom.

SEA TOAD

In some parts of the ocean, The Deep plunges further into the trenches of the **HADAL ZONE** (*hade-il*). More people have ventured into the deepest reaches of space than this part of the ocean. It's another world down here.

Hold your breath – let's meet some of the creatures from The Deep.

STORIES FROM THE DEEP

DEATH PONDS

As life decays it produces a natural gas called **METHANE**, which creates eruptions on the seabed, as though rockets are lifting off. In the Gulf of Mexico these eruptions release a salty liquid called **BRINE** – like the stuff used for pickling vegetables.

Brine is often saltier than the surrounding water, so much so that it is five times heavier, and hovers on the seafloor in these eerie-looking 'ponds'. But don't look too closely –

these ponds are death traps.

The high salt content is toxic to most animals, and those that enter the ponds risk a **squirming** death. But the ponds are tempting too – they're lined with a delicious beach of cold seep mussels that are irresistible to **CUTTHROAT EELS**.

The eels take their chance, and swim into the pond. Some get toxic shock and, in a horrific acrobatic display, twist into knots. One acrobat is caught.

It **twirls**, then **turns**. Will it escape?

With one final squirm, the eel rises out of the brine's deadly hold. It'll live to see another day

LOVE IN A GLASS HOUSE

The Deep hides sunken gardens, with cold-water corals shaped like feathers and trees, and a sponge that appears to be woven from glass – the delicate **VENUS' FLOWER BASKET**.

Here, two **SHRIMP** have been swept away by love.

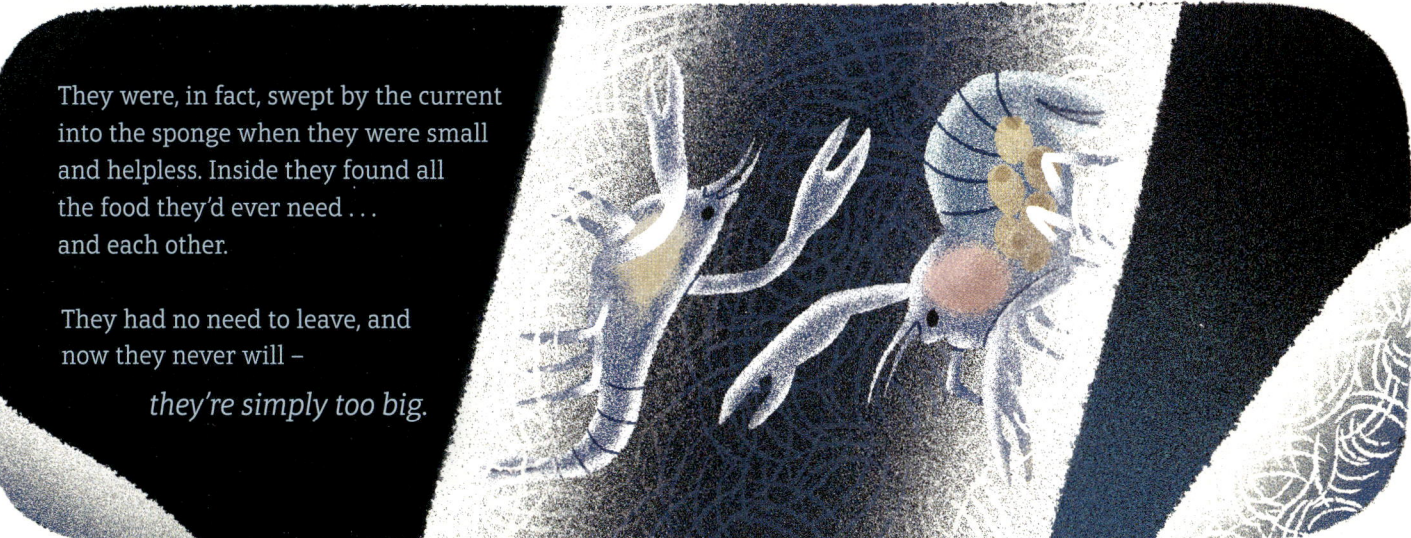

They were, in fact, swept by the current into the sponge when they were small and helpless. Inside they found all the food they'd ever need . . . and each other.

They had no need to leave, and now they never will –

they're simply too big.

But their baby larvae will leave, swimming through the sponge's holes . . .

the whole wide ocean waiting to be explored.

DINNER IS SERVED

When food falls into The Deep, all sorts of creatures scoot and scuttle in the gloom. It's hard to find food down here, so when a decaying **SPERM WHALE**, weighing as much as a lorry, sinks nearly 800 metres down to the seafloor, it causes a feeding frenzy.

BLUNTNOSE SIXGILL SHARKS might only eat once a year, so they **bump** and **barge** like hungry teenagers arriving for dinner.

Within 24 hours a third of the carcass is gone and the ravenous sharks have eaten their fill.

That's when the clean-up crew arrives. **ROCK** and **SPIDER CRABS** join more than 30 species of scavengers to pick the bones clean.

Word of the banquet has reached another deep-sea hunter – the eel-shaped **SCABBARD FISH**. It's almost invisible as it swims upright, coming

closer

and

closer.

It STRIKES

picking off the little scavenger species with its needle-like teeth.

Four months later only the skeleton is left – and that's when the zombies take over. **ZOMBIE WORMS** inject acid to tunnel into the bones and *slurp* up the nutrients inside.

The seabed supper is complete, with not a morsel wasted.

INHABITANTS OF THE DEEP

MY, WHAT BIG EYES YOU HAVE!

Light comes from above, in the dim waters of the Twilight Zone. For many creatures here, the bigger the eyeballs, the better!

The **SWORDFISH** has tennis-ball-sized eyes that heat up – all the better to see you with in the murky depths.

The **BARRELEYE FISH** got its name because its tube-like eyes turn inside its see-through head. Perfect for peering up at potential prey, such as a delicious jellyfish lunch.

The curious **COCKEYED SQUID'S** left eye is twice the size of its right eye. The left eye looks up and the right eye looks down.

WHAT BIG TENTACLES YOU HAVE!

Jelly-like **SIPHONOPHORES** (sigh-fon-oh-fours) are giant trailing death nets. They have stinging tentacles that capture small crustaceans, and they're the longest living thing on the planet. The siphonophore can grow to a whopping forty metres long – that's longer than a blue whale.

At two metres long, the **HUMBOLDT SQUID** is as long as a man is tall. This hungry hunter latches onto its prey with its powerful tentacles and sharp beak.

WHAT BRIGHT LIGHTS YOU HAVE!

Just as fireflies glow on land, many deep-sea creatures use bioluminescence to light up the dim waters of The Deep. Chemical reactions allow these creatures to create lights to scare away predators, lure in a mate – or attract their lunch!

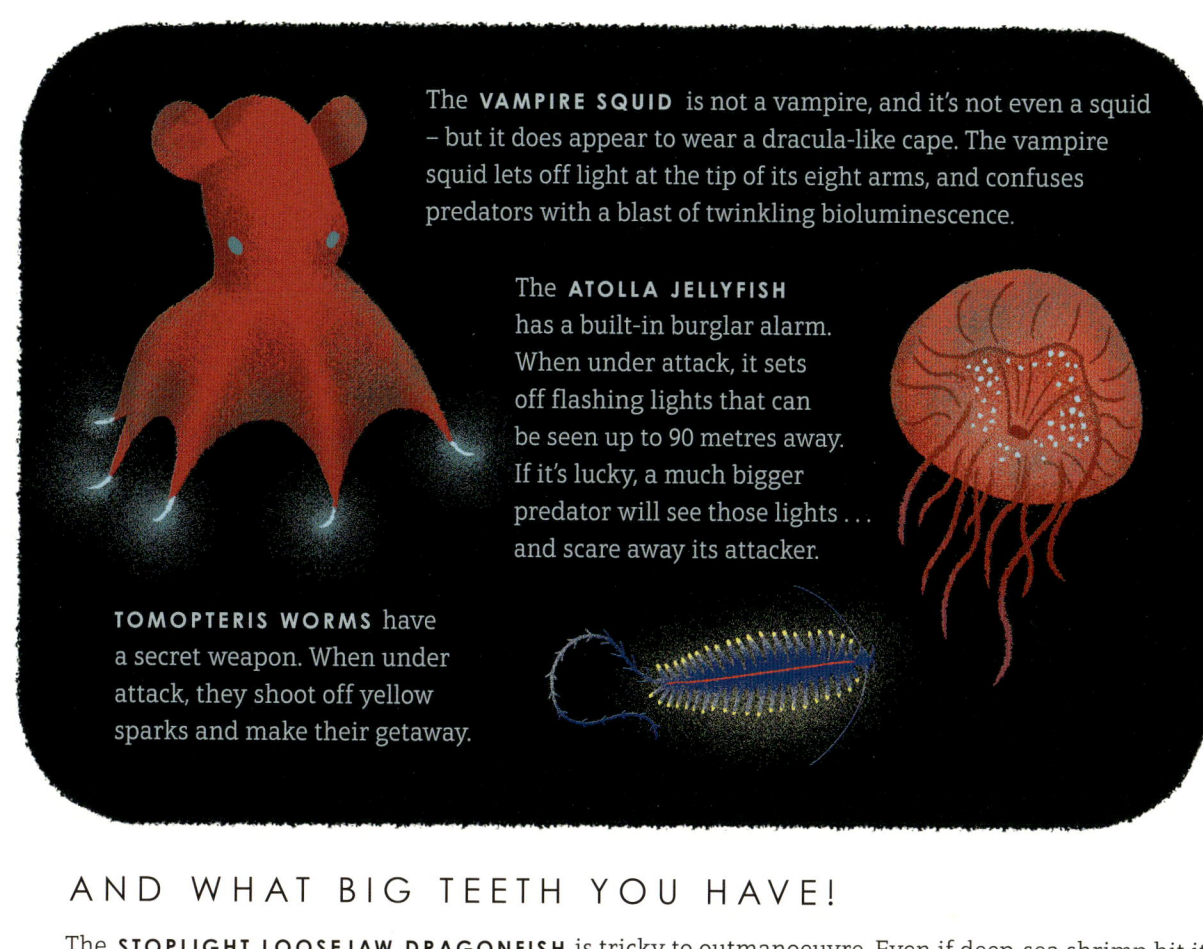

The **VAMPIRE SQUID** is not a vampire, and it's not even a squid – but it does appear to wear a dracula-like cape. The vampire squid lets off light at the tip of its eight arms, and confuses predators with a blast of twinkling bioluminescence.

The **ATOLLA JELLYFISH** has a built-in burglar alarm. When under attack, it sets off flashing lights that can be seen up to 90 metres away. If it's lucky, a much bigger predator will see those lights . . . and scare away its attacker.

TOMOPTERIS WORMS have a secret weapon. When under attack, they shoot off yellow sparks and make their getaway.

AND WHAT BIG TEETH YOU HAVE!

The **STOPLIGHT LOOSEJAW DRAGONFISH** is tricky to outmanoeuvre. Even if deep-sea shrimp hit it with a bioluminescent smokescreen, it simply turns on its red searchlight to scan the area, and attacks with its needle-like teeth.

STOPLIGHT LOOSEJAW DRAGONFISH

The **FANGTOOTH** has frightfully big fangs. They're so long, they have to tuck up into pockets in the roof of its mouth, so it doesn't pierce its brain when its jaws close!

FANGTOOTH

BUT WHAT CUTE FINS YOU HAVE!

FLAPJACK OCTOPUS

Meet **FLAPJACK**, not of the biscuit variety, but the octopus kind. This adorable octopus has stubby tentacles, big wide eyes and earlike fins that it flaps like wings.

LIFE IN THE LOST CITY

Before humans voyaged into The Deep, we wondered if we'd find a sweeping wasteland. Instead, we may have discovered the origin of all life.

Under the ocean's crashing waves, violent volcanoes are at work, tearing apart the ocean floor. As cold seawater seeps through rock cracks towards Earth's fiery centre, it collects minerals and heats up to incredible temperatures. The superhot water then spews back out into the cold ocean, at four times hotter than boiling water (400 degrees Celsius), and forms chimneys called hydrothermal vents. Incredibly, hydrothermal vents can contain as much life as a tropical forest: half a million animals can be crammed into a single square metre.

Beneath the Atlantic Ocean's waves, an area of towering vents has been dubbed the 'Lost City'. Here, scientists have discovered hydrocarbons are being created – molecules that are the building blocks of all life.

They believe life on Earth may have begun around a vent just like this, some four billion years ago. If life can begin and flourish in such extreme conditions down here, perhaps it also exists in the furthest reaches of our galaxy.

CORAL REEFS
WELCOME TO CORAL CITY

Far above The Deep, in shallow, tropical waters, secret cities bustle beneath the waves. Welcome to the ocean's busiest habitat: the world's coral reefs. Flamboyant fish and bright corals make these neon cities shimmer with colour. The neighbourhood is noisy too, with a constant commotion of shrimp snapping, sea urchins scraping and fish crunching.

Schools of fish go with the flow, sweeping over coral ledges, while **SHARKS** and **MANTA RAYS** cruise the waters above.

Knock, knock, who's there? Everyone! Although coral reefs cover just 0.1 per cent of the whole ocean, a quarter of all marine species call them home – with many new species yet to be discovered.

Down here, everyone lives on top of each other. Some animals take up residence in coral mounds as tall as houses. Others prefer hideouts hidden deep within the corals' crevices. And the architects of these vibrant underwater worlds? **CORAL POLYPS** (*pol-ips*) – tiny animals no bigger than a grain of sand.

GREEN TURTLE

CORAL GROUPER

DAY OCTOPUS

Coral polyps get their energy and beautiful colours from **ALGAE** living inside the coral's tissues. They work together: the algae feed the polyp, and the polyp provides a home, one that it constructs a millimetre at a time.

Polyps are hardworking builders that attach themselves to rocks – sometimes multiplying in their thousands – forming colonies of sac-shaped buds, their mouths surrounded by whorls of stinging tentacles.

Hard coral is made when the polyps absorb calcium carbonate (limestone) from the water to build a skeleton. In one year, the slowest growers can gain three millimetres, while the fastest shoot up 100 millimetres (that's only the width of an adult's hand!).

It's no wonder some reefs are millions of years in the making.

STORIES
FROM THE CORAL REEFS

Everyone's got a different job on the reef: from the super-tidy saddleback clownfish which keeps its anemone carpet clean, to the grey reef sharks that patrol the reef's edge. But it's not all hard work in Coral City – some creatures seem to be having the time of their life.

AND . . . RELAX

It's spa time for the **GREEN TURTLES** on Borneo's Turtle Rock. Turtles swim from far and wide so that the little **BLENNIES** and **SURGEONFISH** can pick algae, parasites and dead skin off their shells. The turtles nestle into the rock's hollow, close their eyes and . . .

relax.

But wait, what's all this squabbling?
Some of the turtles are forming a not-so-orderly queue, nipping at each other's flippers. It's a customer service disaster.

In the end, everyone gets their turn.

The fish get fed and the turtles come away looking *turtley* awesome.

CHILD'S PLAY

A family of **BOTTLENOSE DOLPHINS** in the Red Sea are taking a break after a late-night dinner. Mum, Dad and the babies are snoozing, while the teenagers appear to be playing 'Catch the Coral'.

The rules seem to be:

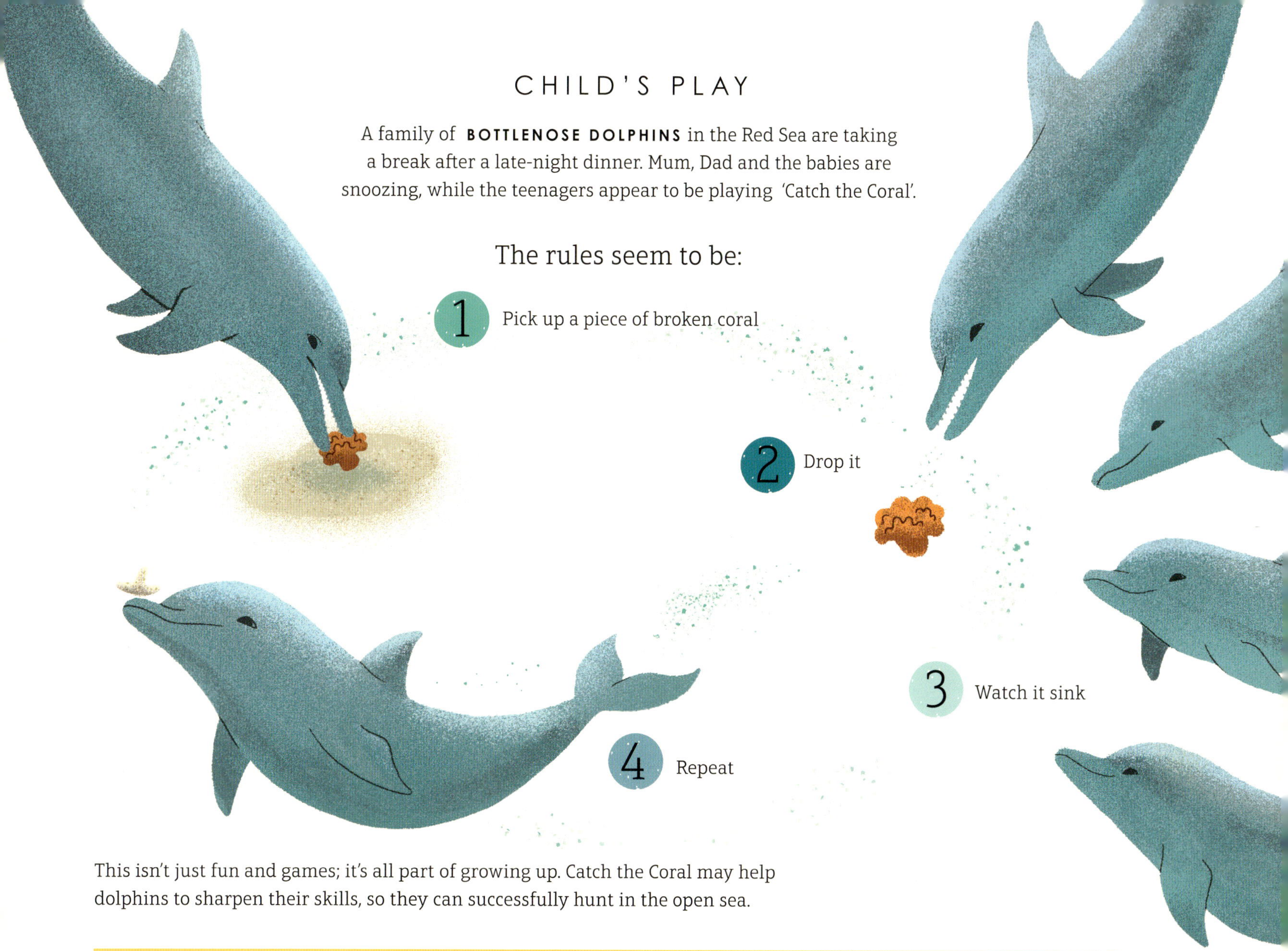

1. Pick up a piece of broken coral
2. Drop it
3. Watch it sink
4. Repeat

This isn't just fun and games; it's all part of growing up. Catch the Coral may help dolphins to sharpen their skills, so they can successfully hunt in the open sea.

TERROR IN THE SUBURBS

Things take a more sinister turn as night falls at the edge of this Indonesian reef. In the open, sandy suburbs, a **LIONFISH** is hunting. It twitches. Perhaps it knows that something is sensing its every move?

It would be right. The giant, carnivorous **BOBBIT WORM** waits, its one-metre-long body buried in the sand and razor-sharp jaws open wide. But the lionfish can't see it. It swims *closer* and *closer*.

Something stirs in the sand. Then...

SNAP!

The bobbit worm **strikes**, pulling the lionfish into its burrow.

The hunter has become the hunted.

INHABITANTS
OF THE CORAL REEF

THE CORAL SKYLINE

Our world's rainbow reefs are home to more than a thousand hard and soft coral species. Hard corals are the backbone of any reef and include brain, staghorn, finger and cauliflower corals. It's not too hard to see how they get their names! But the reef also shimmers and sways with soft corals that look like plants and grasses, including tree coral, carnation coral, toadstool coral and sea fans.

BRAIN CORAL · STAGHORN CORAL · CAULIFLOWER CORAL · FINGER CORAL

CARNATION CORAL · TOADSTOOL CORAL · SEA FAN · TREE CORAL

SMART CEPHALOPODS

Pronounced *seff-uh-low-pods*, these clever invertebrates (animals without a backbone) include octopuses, squid and cuttlefish. Squid and cuttlefish have eight arms plus a pair of feeding tentacles with suckers on their tips. Technically, octopuses have no 'tentacles' but eight short, strong 'arms' with suckers running all the way down.

BROADCLUB CUTTLEFISH

The clever **VEINED OCTOPUS** tiptoes about carrying its own hideout – a coconut husk.

CUTTLEFISH are masters of disguise; their skin changes colour and pattern so they can shape-shift. One minute they look like a rock, the next like a piece of algae. The broadclub cuttlefish even puts on its own lightshow, rapidly changing colour to hypnotize its lunch.

MESMERISING MANTA

With a three-metre wingspan, the graceful **MANTA RAY** moves as effortlessly as a soaring bird, seemingly flying with its wing-like fins. When it's time for lunch, groups of manta ray spiral, creating a whirlpool. This is called 'cyclone feeding'. On a good day, manta rays can eat 27 kilograms of plankton and fish (that's as heavy as the average eight-year-old!).

MANTA RAY

PSYCHEDELIC SLUGS

Some types of **AEOLID** (eh-o-lid) have a sneaky defence. These shell-less molluscs take the stinging cells from the tentacles of anemones, coral and other stinging animals that they eat. Their slime stops them from getting stung, so they can absorb their prey's stings, store them up . . . and then shoot them out when they feel threatened.

CRATENA PEREGRINA

BLUE GLAUCUS

FLABELLINA MACASSARANA

SEA SPITTERS

A **SEA SQUIRT** is a beautiful tube that clings on to coral and rocks. It's a filter feeder, so it sucks water through one opening, filtering out the plankton and other food particles for its dinner, and squirts the leftover water out through another opening. Nervous sea squirts have even been known to shoot out their own stomach!

GOLD-MOUTH SEA SQUIRT

TOOL-WIELDING TUSKFISH

The **ORANGE-DOTTED TUSKFISH** loves to eat clams. But a clam's soft flesh is tucked up inside its tough shell. Luckily, this tuskfish has got just the tool for the job. It grabs the clam in its mouth and swims over to its favourite anvil – a coral head – whacking the clam against it until the shell smashes open. Dinner is served!

ORANGE-DOTTED TUSKFISH

LIFE IN THE BALANCE

For all their flash and flamboyance, our coral cities are fragile. The water needs to be clear and within the right temperature range, so as not to upset the reef's architects – the algae and the coral polyps – who don't like sudden change. Yet sadly the ocean is changing fast.

Polluted freshwater is emptying into the ocean, turning the water cloudy, so there isn't enough sunlight for the coral to grow. And temperature increases are making our oceans much hotter than corals like. These things put stress on corals, and reefs all over the world are dying.

But once a year, the most phenomenal natural event occurs. When a full moon shines down on a calm sea, billions of little colourful balloon-like bundles float towards the ocean's surface. The corals are spawning. All at once, they release an egg bundle that's swept away on the current. As the eggs are fertilized to become larvae, they drift across the ocean looking for a new coral city to call home.

If we can prevent our oceans from getting any warmer, then the coral will continue to spawn, giving us hope that even reefs that are now rubble might still be reborn.

GREEN SEAS
UNDERWATER FORESTS AND GARDENS

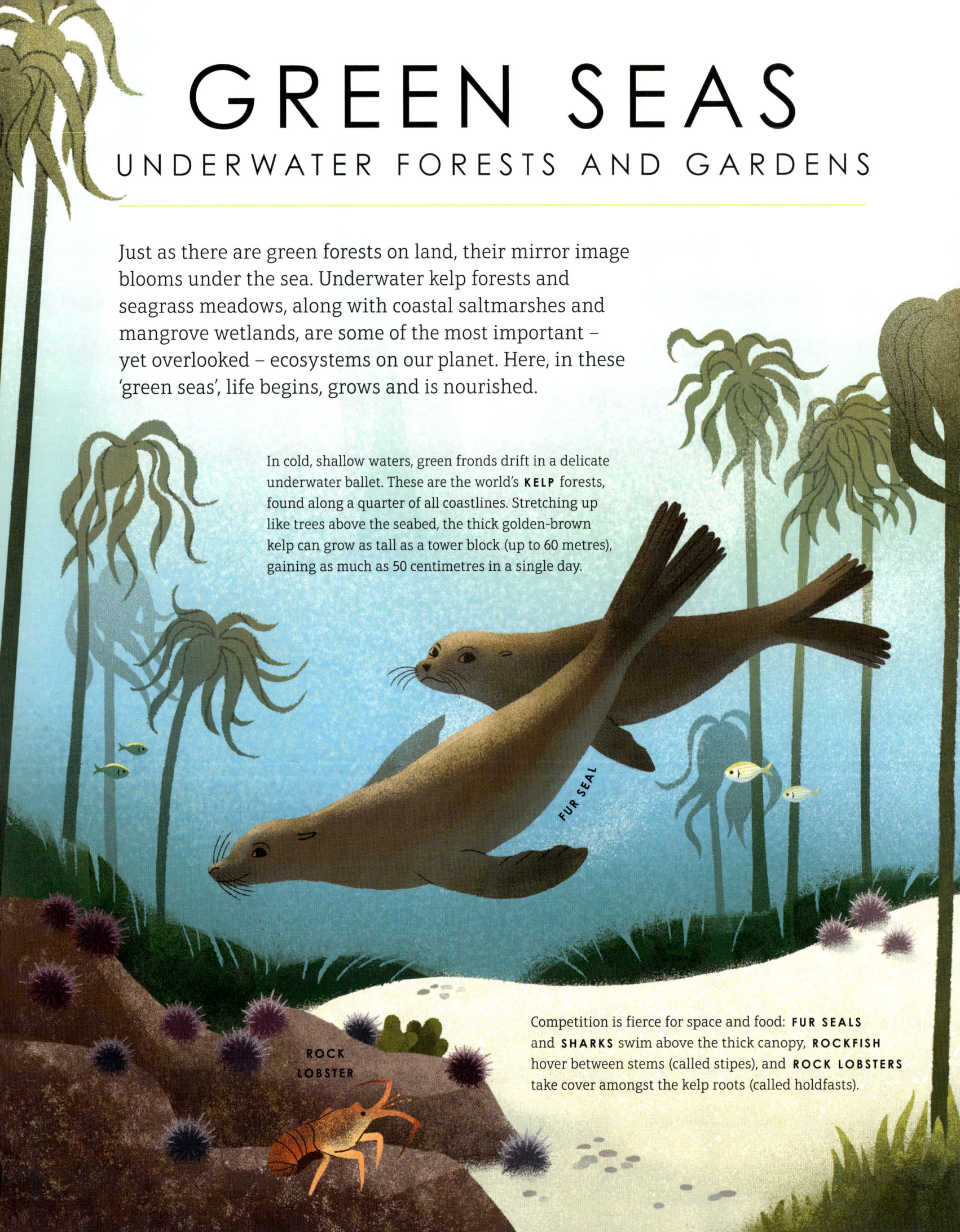

Just as there are green forests on land, their mirror image blooms under the sea. Underwater kelp forests and seagrass meadows, along with coastal saltmarshes and mangrove wetlands, are some of the most important – yet overlooked – ecosystems on our planet. Here, in these 'green seas', life begins, grows and is nourished.

In cold, shallow waters, green fronds drift in a delicate underwater ballet. These are the world's **KELP** forests, found along a quarter of all coastlines. Stretching up like trees above the seabed, the thick golden-brown kelp can grow as tall as a tower block (up to 60 metres), gaining as much as 50 centimetres in a single day.

Competition is fierce for space and food: **FUR SEALS** and **SHARKS** swim above the thick canopy, **ROCKFISH** hover between stems (called stipes), and **ROCK LOBSTERS** take cover amongst the kelp roots (called holdfasts).

Another important green seas habitat can be found from the Tropics to the Arctic: flowering **SEAGRASS MEADOWS**. They stretch along the ocean floor like prairie grasslands. In these sunlit waters you might spot **GREEN TURTLES** and **DUGONGS** as they munch away, keeping the grasses trim and healthy.

While seagrass meadows can be vital nurseries for young fish, some of the richest nurseries can be found elsewhere in the green seas: in coastal **SALTMARSHES** and **MANGROVE FORESTS**. They fringe the coastlines, and baby fish hide from hungry predators within the tangle of grass, roots and leaves.

PYJAMA SHARK

Our green seas – kelp forests, seagrass meadows, saltmarshes and mangrove forests – are some of the most crowded underwater worlds. Together they help to feed marine life across our Blue Planet.

COMMON OCTOPUS

STORIES
FROM THE GREEN SEAS

MUNCH, MUNCH, URCHIN LUNCH

Most of the time **SEA OTTERS** hunt alone, but sometimes they come together in giant rafts to rest. Scientists have spotted over a thousand sea otters floating together, kelp tied around their bodies, so they're anchored to the seabed. They float on their backs, nose and toes pointed into the air. **Bliss.**

But can you hear that sound? *Munch, munch, munch.* In North America's Pacific kelp forests, a huge group of **SEA URCHINS** carpet the seafloor, their spiky bodies looking like pincushions.

Their rabbit-like teeth are razor sharp, and they have overrun this kelp forest, eating through the kelp's roots and setting the kelp adrift. **Someone needs to get these urchins under control.**

Luckily, a team of eager sea otters comes to the rescue! These teddy bears of the sea have a huge appetite and they like to munch on sea urchins. They can help to keep urchin numbers down and kelp forests healthy.

HIDE-O-PUS OCTOPUS

One, two, three... ready or not, here shark comes!

A hungry **PYJAMA SHARK** is patrolling South Africa's kelp forest, peering through the canopy. It wants tentacles for tea.

This **COMMON OCTOPUS** has found itself in an unwelcome game of hide-and-seek.

Luckily, the very clever octopus is the king of camouflage. It builds a suit of armour out of shells and stones and stays very ... *very* ... still.

The shark swims past. A wide eye peeks open from the pile of shells. And, in a puff of ink ...

... the clever octopus makes its escape!

SPIDER-CRAB SCRUM

With a *click, click* sound, hundreds of thousands of **SPIDER CRABS** scuttle through Australia's seagrass meadows. They climb on top of each other, forming great mounds nearly 100 metres long. These crabs have gathered for a costume change! The crabs are growing, so they need to break out of their current shell. Underneath is a roomier soft shell, which will harden up in a few days, but for now the spider crabs are exposed.

Hungry **STINGRAYS** swoop in. Some crabs scatter, but there's strength in numbers, in the safety of the scrum.

INHABITANTS
OF THE GREEN SEAS

FE, FI, FO – KELP!

Creatures living in kelp forests must feel like they're surrounded by giant, magical beanstalks! Gas-filled bladders keep the kelp upright in the water and it grows fast, shooting skywards, spreading across the water in a thick canopy.

A MANTIS MATCH

It's not a zebra. It's not a mantis. It's not even a shrimp. It's a lightning-fast **ZEBRA MANTIS SHRIMP** – and it's one of the green seas' deadliest predators. As long as a four-year-old's leg, the zebra mantis shrimp is also a fantastic partner. The male drags fish into his burrow for his hungry mate, as she prepares to lay their eggs. Some mantis couples stay together for 20 years.

WEEDY SEADRAGON

HERE BE DRAGONS

Is it a leaf? Is it a seahorse? No, it's a **WEEDY SEADRAGON**! With a long snout and tail and leafy limbs, the seadragon is perfectly disguised to blend in among the seaweed and kelp.

ZEBRA MANTIS SHRIMP

THE GREAT GARIBALDI GARDENER

The bright orange **GARIBALDI** is a very cranky gardener. When it's time to nest with a female, he busily tends to his home turf. The seaweed's hedged, the algae's trimmed, and unwanted guests... are swiftly dealt with. Snails are carted off one by one, and there are strictly **NO URCHINS ALLOWED!**

GARIBALDI

GIANT KELP

A gorgeous garden will help him to woo the female, encouraging her to lay eggs in his garden patch.

PROWLING THE MEADOWS

Just as big cats roam the African plains, **TIGER SHARKS** patrol Australia's seagrass meadows. Some can grow longer than a car, and they get their name from the grey stripes on their powerful bodies.

GREEN TURTLES eat almost two kilograms of seagrass a day, working like underwater lawnmowers. And with tiger sharks about, the turtles are always on the move, keeping the seabed nice and trim.

WHERE THE RIVER MEETS THE SEA

Mangrove forests are found in tidal waters. The trees grow roots above the ground that work like snorkels to help them breathe as the tide comes and goes. Some are pencil, peg, or knee-like prop roots that are covered in pores, just like human skin.

BEAUTIES AND THE BEASTS

Baby fish such as **GOLIATH GROUPER** hide from bigger fish, **CROCODILES** and **BIRDS** in the muddy roots of mangrove swamps.

SUPERHERO SEAS

Our green seas are in trouble. They're being cleared and built on for our towns and cities, and choked by pollution. Rising sea levels mean less life-giving sunlight reaches the plants on the seafloor – and they need light to grow. The health of these underwater forests matters to us all.

Seagrass meadows, kelp and mangrove forests, and tidal marshes capture and store surprising amounts of carbon, helping to reduce CO_2 in the atmosphere that adds to global warming. And the humble plants of our green seas feed life, all the way up the food chain. The green seas feed microscopic plankton, which feeds the herbivores, who feed the ocean's mightiest and toothiest predators. Our green seas are the superheroes of the sea. And just like our forests on land, our beautiful forests in the sea need our protection.

COASTS
EVER-CHANGING WORLDS

Between the land and the sea is a wild, ever-changing place that cannot be tamed – the coast. At the mercy of constant pounding waves and shifting sands, the coast is where worlds collide.

Swollen high-tide water gives way to the low tide, revealing hidden wonderlands in rockpools and shores.

To survive, many creatures walk the line between these high and low water worlds – but they mustn't dawdle, because their world changes as swiftly as the tides.

BROWN ALGAE

OCHRE SEA STAR

LIMPET

Waves begin far out at sea, getting stronger and stronger as they roll into shore. They're the great sculptors of the sea, carving towering fortresses and dramatic arches. Even the gentlest ripples chip away at the shore, one grain at a time.

As the tide goes out, it reveals windswept beaches, stony shorelines and rockpool oases. In these low-tide worlds, only the toughest survive.

GIANT GREEN ANEMONE

BLUE MUSSEL

SEA LEMON

BLUEBAND HERMIT CRAB

First battered by waves, then left high and dry at low tide, life here has learned to adapt. For a few hours each day it's rockpool rush hour, as coastal creatures slide, scamper and squelch, eating their fill before the tide returns.

This is the curious world of our coasts.

STORIES FROM THE COAST

ELEPHANT-SEAL SQUABBLE

On the shores of the sub-Antarctic island of South Georgia, this bull **SOUTHERN ELEPHANT SEAL** is the beachmaster. Weighing as much as eight grand pianos, this steaming wall of blubber likes to snooze with his girlfriends. But these **KING PENGUINS** need to get past. With so many sleeping giants, they can't go over them, they can't go under them.

Carefully, the penguins tiptoe through them.

Suddenly there's a guttural gurgle. The bull boss is awake. And another bull is galloping in – he's come to challenge the beachmaster. Oh dear, the penguins are caught in the crossfire.

The penguins go left, right, trying to swiftly patter past.

With each **thwack, wallop** and **bite**, the ground shakes.

Finally, the beachmaster reigns supreme, and in all the commotion, the penguins quickly flip-flap past.

CATCH A CRAB

These nimble **SALLY LIGHTFOOT CRABS** are limbering up. As the tide goes out, their algae feeding ground is revealed 100 metres from shore. It's time for their daily dash across the rocks to reach the algae. If they look like scaredy crabs, that's because they are. All that lies between the crabs and lunch is . . . a handful of slippery predators. There's always something lurking in the water.

Ready, set . . . go, crabs, GO!
The crabs make a run for it, leaping from rock to rock, careful not to touch the water.

A **CHAIN MORAY EEL** erupts from the shallows – but it misses the crabs and belly-flops back into the water.

Splash!

A panicked crab slips into a pool.
Swim, Sally Lightfoot, swim!
It clambers up slippery rocks – but nowhere is safe.

An octopus creeps from a crevice, body slapping across the rocks.

IT'S BEHIND YOU, SALLY LIGHTFOOT!

The crab scuttles, but just as it leaps on to a rock . . . an eel grabs its leg. Is this the end? No! Luckily, with a wriggle and a jiggle, the crab finally breaks free.

Eat up, Sally Lightfoot, you'll do it all again in a few hours, before the tide returns.

ADRIFT IN THE ICY BLUE

Walruses live at the top of the world, in the Arctic's icy ocean. It's a world that's melting. Warming sea temperatures are reducing the thick sea ice where the walrus mothers once safely raised their pups.

As the thinner sea ice crumbles under their weight, hundreds of quarrelsome walrus mothers are forced to take their chance on dry land.

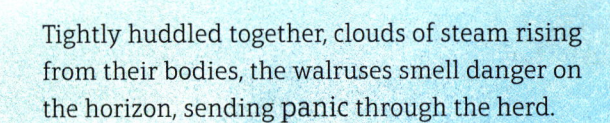

Tightly huddled together, clouds of steam rising from their bodies, the walruses smell danger on the horizon, sending panic through the herd.

Polar bears.

They've young to feed too, and the walrus calves are in danger.

The herd bellow to raise the alarm, and *frantically* clamber into the sea – jostling for the little ice that's left.

But the ice floes are becoming fewer and further away –

it's a desperate swim to safety.

One mother's head bobs above the water, searching for space as her exhausted calf slips beneath the waves. She cradles the calf in her flippers to try and keep it afloat, but it's tired.

Exhausted, the mother and calf finally find an empty ice floe. Just in time. With one last push, they haul themselves out and flop on to the ice.

Safe for the moment, together.

INHABITANTS
OF THE COASTS

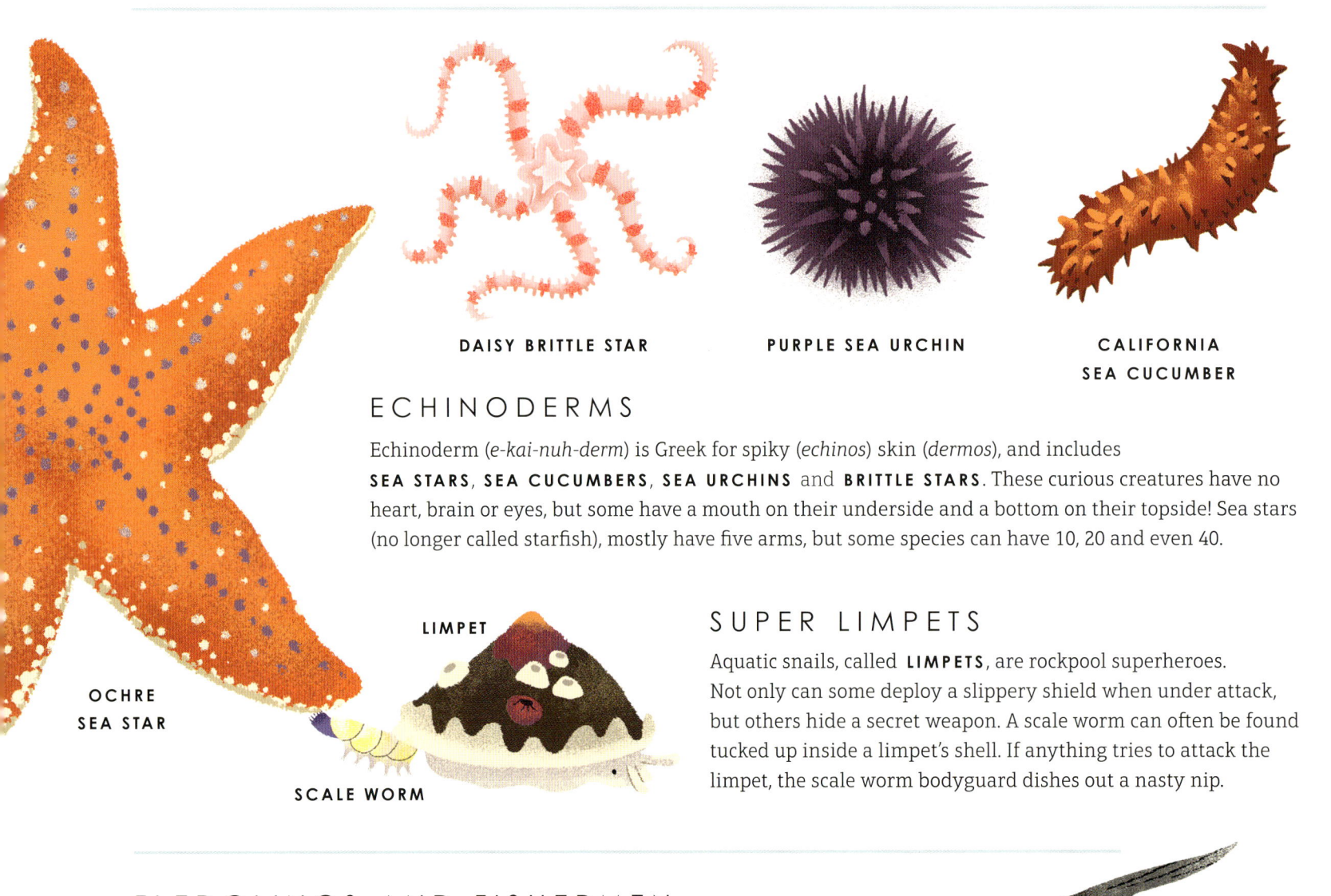

DAISY BRITTLE STAR

PURPLE SEA URCHIN

CALIFORNIA SEA CUCUMBER

ECHINODERMS

Echinoderm (*e-kai-nuh-derm*) is Greek for spiky (*echinos*) skin (*dermos*), and includes **SEA STARS**, **SEA CUCUMBERS**, **SEA URCHINS** and **BRITTLE STARS**. These curious creatures have no heart, brain or eyes, but some have a mouth on their underside and a bottom on their topside! Sea stars (no longer called starfish), mostly have five arms, but some species can have 10, 20 and even 40.

OCHRE SEA STAR

LIMPET

SCALE WORM

SUPER LIMPETS

Aquatic snails, called **LIMPETS**, are rockpool superheroes. Not only can some deploy a slippery shield when under attack, but others hide a secret weapon. A scale worm can often be found tucked up inside a limpet's shell. If anything tries to attack the limpet, the scale worm bodyguard dishes out a nasty nip.

FLEDGLINGS AND FISHERMEN

Week-old **ATLANTIC PUFFINS** are hungry little hatchlings – they need to eat five times a day. That makes Mum and Dad keen fishermen, flying up to 50 kilometres out to sea and plunging as far as 40 metres beneath the waves to fetch their fish supper.

ATLANTIC PUFFIN

ARCTIC SKUA

PIRATES OF THE SEA

ARCTIC SKUAS steal most of what they eat. As seabirds such as puffins and guillemots finish a day's fishing and fly home to their nests, the skuas strike! They fly low and fast over the waves to ambush the birds, stealing their catch.

PLUCKY PENGUINS

There are eighteen types of penguin and they nearly all live in the southern hemisphere (except for Galapagos penguins that live just north of the Equator). These flightless birds have flippers instead of wings so, even though they're clumsy on land, they're speedy in the sea.

Antarctica's **EMPEROR PENGUINS** are hardy survivors, known to endure temperatures as low as minus 40 degrees Celsius by tightly huddling in groups. They're tall too, reaching the height of an average six-year-old.

CHINSTRAP PENGUIN

GENTOO PENGUIN

EMPEROR PENGUIN

CHINSTRAP PENGUINS get their name from the band of black feathers that run under their chin.

GENTOO penguins can dive 450 times a day and swim three times faster than an Olympic front crawl swimmer.

PACIFIC LEAPING BLENNY

A FISH OUT OF WATER

The eight-centimetre-long **PACIFIC LEAPING BLENNY** fish spends most of its life out of the water. The male ventures a metre above the low-tide line – it must feel like scaling a cliff. Here, he makes his nest amongst the delicious algae. But he needs to grab the attention of the grazing female blenny below, so she'll climb up to lay her eggs. A flash of his fetching orange fin ought to do it!

WORLDS COLLIDING

Today millions of humans crowd our coastlines. Long before we flocked there, animals gathered along our wild shores – and they still do.

On Florida's Palm Beach, throngs of tourists share the sea with ten thousand blacktip and spinner sharks. It's one of the biggest shark get-togethers on the planet as they rest before their journey north.

For every soaring cliff on our coastline, there are skyscraper buildings. And for each sandy stretch of beach there's an endless shopping centre. It's no longer enough for coastal creatures to manage the tricky worlds of low and high tide. They must also learn to cope with our human world, with its pollution and constant development. Our worlds are colliding, but it's not too late for humans and nature to live in harmony.

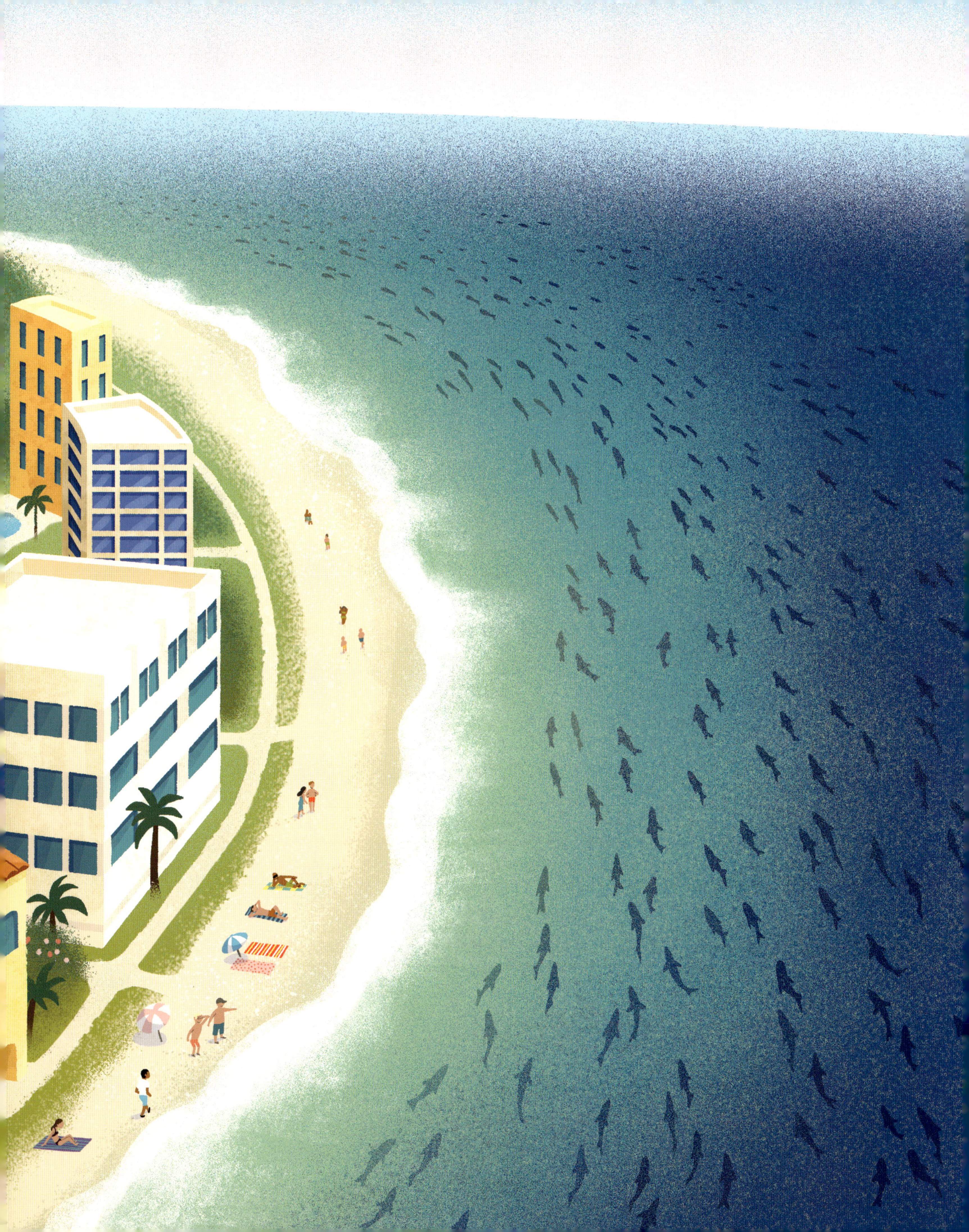

BIG BLUE
OCEANIC OUTBACK

The greatest wilderness on our planet isn't at the top of a mountain, it's in the open ocean of the Big Blue.

Far from the bustling shoreline, the Big Blue is an oceanic desert – vast and seemingly empty. Here, meals can be few and far between. But every so often the Big Blue explodes with life, as news of huge schools of fish brings some of the ocean's biggest predators out in number.

SPINNER DOLPHIN

The sparseness of the Big Blue can provide a safe haven for the ocean's young. With flippers moving fast, green turtle hatchlings head from the crowded coast for the open sea. A simple floating log becomes an offshore refuge, where the turtles can dine on tiny algae, barnacles and crustaceans. But they'll need to be on the lookout . . . even here big predators are never too far away.

GREEN TURTLE

Large mammals, such as whales and dolphins, migrate across the ocean, travelling great distances to eat their fill. Speedier sharks and those true ocean sprinters, the sailfish, slice through the water, moving in on the catch of the day.

In this incredible habitat, thousands of kilometres from land, both the ocean's youngest and biggest inhabitants begin their epic voyages across the Big Blue.

STORIES
FROM THE BIG BLUE

SLEEPING GIANTS

The mother **SPERM WHALE** is resting, nose down, tail up – as if standing in the ocean. Together with the other females in her pod, she can stay like this for fifteen minutes.

Motionless and majestic.

But this morning there's no time to rest – her hungry calf wants milk. The mother reluctantly opens a sleepy eye. She needs to eat to make milk for her calf. She dives, just like a submarine, *down, down, down* into the dark, using sonar to hunt for a shoal of squid . . .

click,

click,

click.

As the mother dives deeper, her clicks get faster.

Click

click

click

click

click.

Then silence.
Breakfast has begun.

With a tummy full of squid, the mother returns to the surface in time for her calf to enjoy its milk.

BLOOMING WONDERFUL

Everyone's on the move to Monterey Bay on America's west coast.

As summer sunshine touches the water, the sea blooms with clouds of tiny algae called **PHYTOPLANKTON**. Millions of **ANCHOVIES** have come to feast and hot on their tails are hungry **DOLPHINS** and **SEA LIONS**. **SEABIRDS** dive bomb and everyone races to eat their fill.

Then... a deep groan rumbles beneath the waves. There's a *thunderous* breach...

...as a giant **HUMPBACK WHALE** explodes from the water.

Water cascades over its barnacled back as up to *100 kilograms* of fish is sieved through its baleen (mouth bristles), weighing almost as much as the dolphins speeding past.

The microscopic algae have set off a chain reaction, creating a massive sea migration that will feed life across the ocean.

INHABITANTS
OF THE BIG BLUE

OCEAN BRUISERS AND CRUISERS

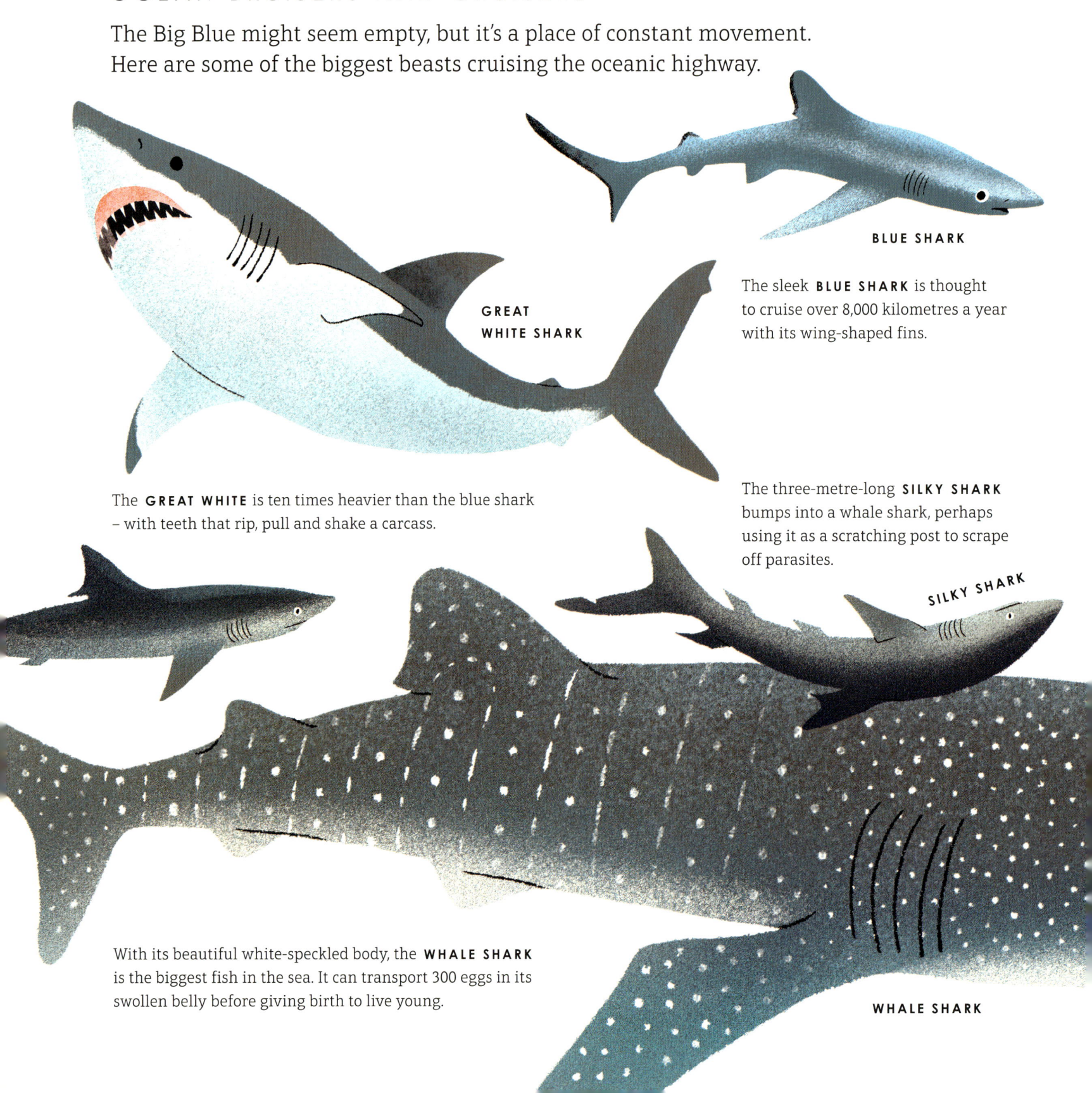

The Big Blue might seem empty, but it's a place of constant movement. Here are some of the biggest beasts cruising the oceanic highway.

GREAT WHITE SHARK

BLUE SHARK

The sleek **BLUE SHARK** is thought to cruise over 8,000 kilometres a year with its wing-shaped fins.

The **GREAT WHITE** is ten times heavier than the blue shark – with teeth that rip, pull and shake a carcass.

The three-metre-long **SILKY SHARK** bumps into a whale shark, perhaps using it as a scratching post to scrape off parasites.

SILKY SHARK

With its beautiful white-speckled body, the **WHALE SHARK** is the biggest fish in the sea. It can transport 300 eggs in its swollen belly before giving birth to live young.

WHALE SHARK

NOMADIC CNIDARIAN

The name cnidarian (*nigh-dair-ree-an*) means 'stinging creature', so within this animal group you can find jellyfish, siphonophores and sea anemones. Jellyfish can cross an entire ocean feeding on whatever is entangled in the stingers that trail behind them.

Some jellyfish look psychedelic, such as the **MOON JELLYFISH** – rising and pulsing through the water like bubbles in a lava lamp. Other cnidarians send a shiver through your spine.

The **PORTUGUESE MAN O' WAR** looks like a jellyfish but is a siphonophore – a colony of small bodies attached together. It hoists up its iridescent sail and rides the waves like a deadly yacht, tentacles trailing behind it. This lethal fishing line stings and paralyses its prey, which are reeled in, liquified with powerful chemicals and then digested.

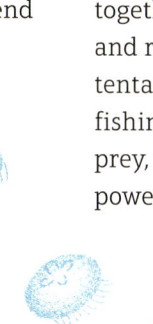

MOON JELLYFISH

PORTUGUESE MAN O' WAR

FILL UP ON PLANKTON

Plankton is made up of tiny plants (phytoplankton) and tiny animals (zooplankton). From space, **PHYTOPLANKTON** blooms look like turquoise ink splodges spreading across the water. These microscopic algae use sunlight to grow. **ZOOPLANKTON** (tiny fish, krill and jellyfish) will eat the phytoplankton, then bigger predators will eat the zooplankton. In this way, tiny phytoplankton set off a chain reaction, as they feed life all the way up the ocean food chain.

WANDERING ALBATROSS

THE SAT NAV ALBATROSS

The **WANDERING ALBATROSS** has the biggest wingspan of any bird on the planet: it is 3.5 metres which is twice as wide as some cars. Better yet, it's got sat nav built into its brain to help guide it to the same nest site year after year. Each year some 2,500 wandering albatrosses return to the island of South Georgia, in the Southern Atlantic Ocean, where many raise fluffy white chicks.

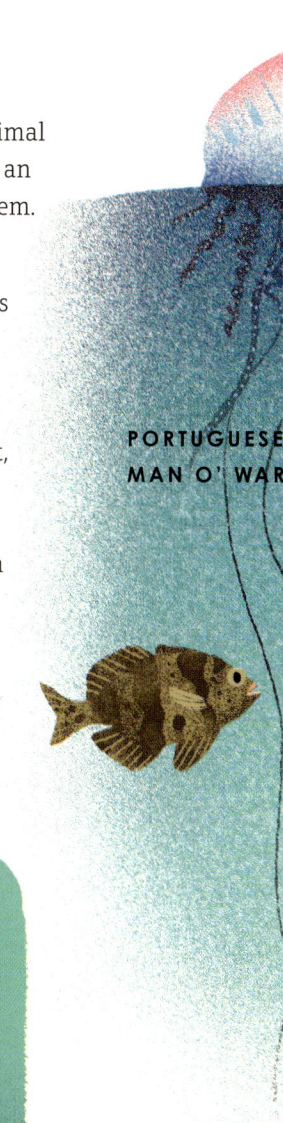

NOWHERE TO HIDE

While it's hard to imagine that a watery wilderness so vast, deep and unexplored could feel the impact of our human world . . . it has. From warming seas and overfishing to ocean pollution, we're putting the health of our oceans under threat.

Around eight million metric tons of plastic washes into the ocean each year; the equivalent of a full garbage truckload every minute. It twists around fins, necks and beaks, drowning many marine creatures. Weathered by the sun and waves, it breaks down into confetti-sized pieces, or even smaller into tiny glitter-sized microplastics (less than five millimetres) which float on the water's surface or wash up onshore. Mistaken for food, they're swallowed by more than 220 marine species – from seabirds and fish to crustaceans. The effects are felt through the food chain, right to the very top. Us. Without even knowing it, we might consume thousands of microplastic pieces each year in the marine life we eat. We're polluting the ocean at our peril.

But we're also changing.

We're saying no to single-use plastic. We're reusing and recycling. We're working together to protect the ocean. After all, this Blue Planet is the only home for nearly eight billion humans, and an uncountable number of other species – with new ones discovered every day. It's a home worth protecting.

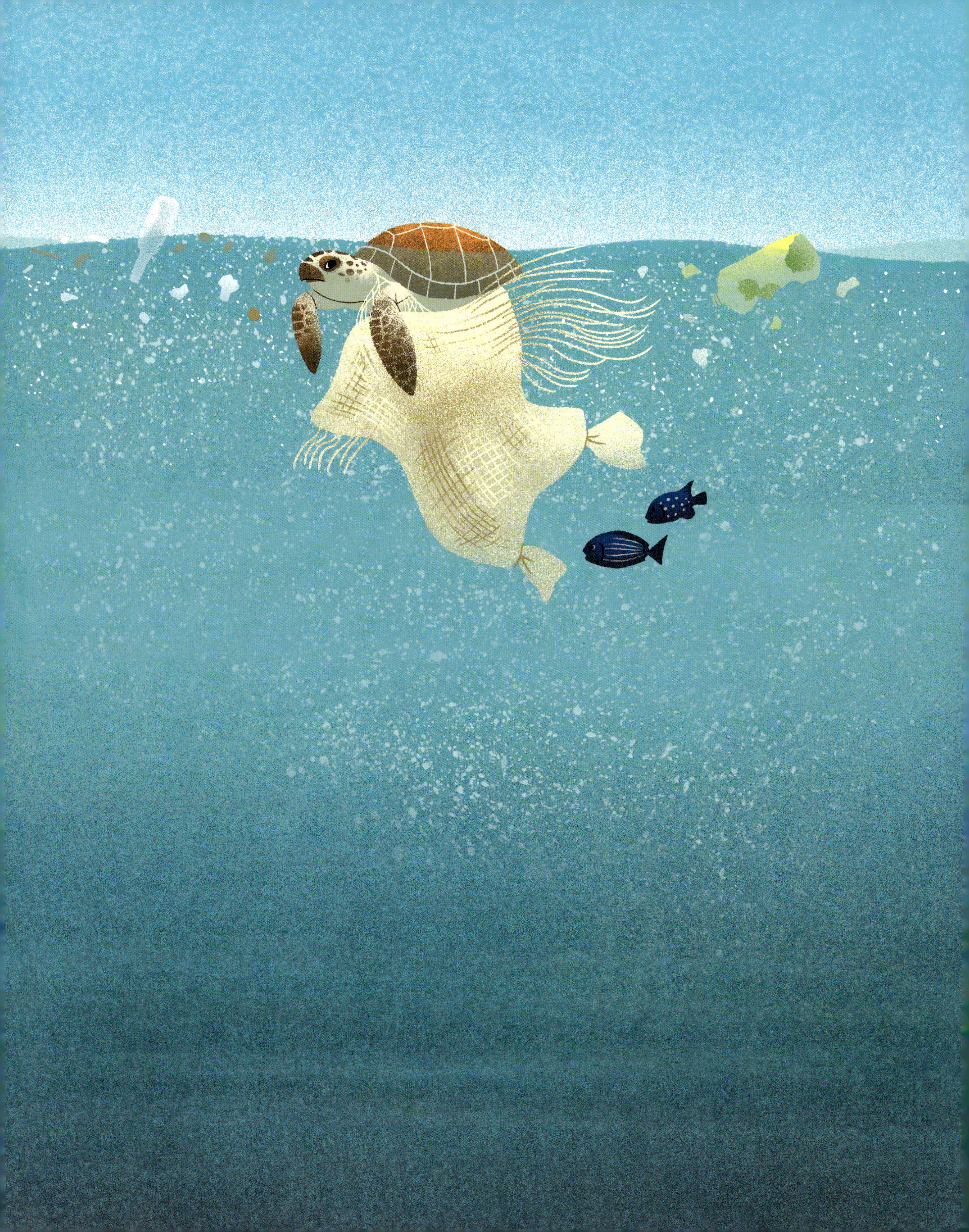

CALLING ALL
OCEAN HEROES

Around the world there are humans who care deeply about protecting our planet. And there are heroes who are devoting their lives to safeguarding our seas. Here are just a few of the ways scientists are learning more about our ocean, so we can make our blue spaces better places.

LISTENING

Dr Steve Simpson has learned that fish chat all day long, making sounds to scare off predators or attract a partner. This is an underwater language we're only just beginning to understand, and Steve is working with his underwater microphone to listen in on the extraordinary chomping, crunching and crackling underwater. As seas get busier with the din of boat propellers and offshore drilling, it's harder for fish to be heard and for baby fish to find a reef to make their home. But the more we understand the impact we're having, the sooner we can turn the volume down.

TRACKING

Scientists use tracking devices to follow animals and learn about their behaviours – from where they feed to how far they travel for food. Zoologist Dr Lucy Quinn used trackers to discover why wandering albatross numbers are declining on one of their main nesting sites, the small island of South Georgia near Antarctica. She found adult albatrosses are mistakenly carrying plastic from far out at sea back to the nest as food for their chicks.

Scientists are now trying to understand how eating plastic might affect the albatrosses, while tracking data might help to find plastic hotspots in the sea.

EXPLORING

With so much ocean waiting to be explored, Dr Jon Copley makes daring deep-sea dives in a minisubmarine to uncover what secrets are hiding on the ocean floor. He's witnessed unexpected life in Antarctica's near-freezing waters, from new creatures in hydrothermal vents, like the hairy-chested yeti crab, to giant sponges that grow as much as two metres high.

It's thanks to these missions that scientists are able to spotlight new creatures and habitats that need our protection.

PROTECTING

Numbers of the world's largest turtle, the leatherback, have declined catastrophically over the years. But on the Caribbean island of Trinidad, there is hope. A few decades ago, leatherback eggs were stolen, and the turtles sold for meat or leather. Then, conservationist Len Peters appointed himself turtle bodyguard. Each night Len patrolled his village beach to protect the nests. Together with the local community, he has helped change the turtles fortune. In 1990 just 30 nesting leatherbacks visited Len's beach and a nearby bay, each night.

Today, around 500 leatherbacks haul up to lay their eggs – a victory for conservation!

YOUR BLUE PLANET

There are simple things that we can all do, every day, to help protect our Blue Planet.

POWER DOWN

See if you can reduce your energy usage: next time you feel chilly, try layering up rather than turning up the heating. Switch off lights when you're not in a room, and unplug electronics when you're not using them. These actions will use less energy, so there'll be less carbon dioxide (CO_2) in the air that makes Earth warmer.

THE LUNGS OF OUR PLANET

Trees can take in CO_2 and breathe out oxygen. The more trees we plant, the more we can protect our planet from global warming.

BECOME A SEA-LIFE SPOTTER

You can help scientists understand what's happening to wildlife populations. From bird-spotting to fish and mammal tracking, or counting different seaweeds found on the beach, together we can help gather new information.

PLASTIC IS NOT FANTASTIC

Rubbish that's left on the ground can wash into drains, flush into the sea and be eaten by wildlife. And plastic can take hundreds of years to break down. That's why, all over the world, countries are beginning to ban single-use plastics such as carrier bags.

REDUCE, REUSE, RECYCLE

Try reducing the amount of plastic you use by carrying a reusable water bottle and saying no to plastic straws. Rather than throwing things away, we can share with others, so that old toys and clothes can become new again. Those things that can't be reduced or reused can be carefully recycled. This keeps them out of landfill so they can be born again: cardboard boxes can become paper, fruit and vegetable peelings can be composted into soil.

Seen from space, Earth at night twinkles like the stars in the galaxy all around us. Today, the web of lights shines brighter, glowing where once it was dark, as our footprints extend across the planet. But with each new day, more of us are finding ways to tread lightly on our planet.

Change begins in this way – like a ripple far out at sea that turns into a wave, growing bigger, and gathering power, as it thunders into shore.